Collins

11+

Verbal Reasoning Cloze

Practice Workbook

Angela Marks

T0317904

Contents

ACKNOWLEDGEMENTS

The author and publisher are grateful to the copyright holders for permission to use quoted materials and images.

Every effort has been made to trace copyright holders and obtain their permission for the use of copyright material. The author and publisher will gladly receive information enabling them to rectify any error or omission in subsequent editions. All facts are correct at time of going to press.

Published by Collins
An imprint of HarperCollinsPublishers
1 London Bridge Street
London SE1 9GF

HarperCollinsPublishers
1st Floor, Watermarque Building,
Ringsend Road, Dublin 4, Ireland

ISBN: 9781844199006

First published 2016

This edition published 2020

Previously published by Letts

10 9

© HarperCollinsPublishers Limited 2020

All rights reserved. No part of this publication may be reproduced, stored in a retrieval system, or transmitted, in any form or by any means, electronic, mechanical, photocopying, recording or otherwise, without the prior permission of Collins.

British Library Cataloguing in Publication Data.

A CIP record of this book is available from the British Library.

Author: Angela Marks
Commissioning Editor: Michelle I'Anson
Editor and Project Manager: Sonia Dawkins
Cover Design: Kevin Robbins and Sarah Duxbury
Text Design, Layout and Artwork: Q2A Media
Production: Lyndsey Rogers
Printed in the United Kingdom

Please note that Collins is not associated with CEM in any way. This book does not contain any official questions and it is not endorsed by CEM.

Our question types are based on those set by CEM, but we cannot guarantee that your child's actual 11+ exam will contain the same question types or format as this book.

Guidance for Parents

About the 11+ tests

In most cases, the 11+ selection tests are set by GL Assessment (NFER), CEM or the individual school. You should be able to find out which tests your child will be taking on the website of the school they are applying to, or from the local authority.

The CEM test consists of two papers and in each paper pupils are tested on their abilities in verbal, non-verbal and numerical reasoning. Tests are separated into small, timed sections delivered by audio instructions. It appears the content required for CEM tests changes from year to year, and the level at which pupils are tested ranges from county to county.

For pupils to do well in the CEM tests:

- They must have strong arithmetic skills
- They must have strong reasoning and problem-solving skills
- They must have a strong core vocabulary
- They must be flexible and able to understand and respond to a wide range of question types and formats, without being panicked by unfamiliar question types
- They must be able to work under time pressure.

About this book

This book provides preparation for the verbal reasoning aspect of the exam and, more specifically, for cloze testing. These types of tests present passages with a number of words omitted. Children must correctly fill in the blanks. Cloze tests assess children's vocabulary, reading comprehension and contextual understanding of a passage.

This book contains:

- 60 tests focused on building cloze skills
- Top tips for managing time and using it to best effect
- Interesting facts and ideas for extension activities throughout
- A complete set of answers
- A score sheet to track results over multiple attempts.

How to use this book

We suggest that your child writes the answers on a separate piece of paper when attempting the tests for the first time, as you may want your child to complete them again at a later date. You should record your child's first attempt at each test in the table at the end of the book. At a later date, your child should repeat any section where the score was poor or where they were unable to finish. The time allowed for each test is set to be challenging, but eventually manageable for your child.

Depending on the amount of practice of timed tests which your child has completed prior to using this book, initially your child may find the tests difficult to complete. However, it is through practice of timed tests that children gain more confidence and become more time-aware. Writing answers on a separate piece of paper allows the tests to be re-used.

Your child will need:

- A quiet place to do the tests
- A clock/watch which is visible to your child
- A piece of paper (on which to write the answers)
- A pencil.

Cloze Wordbank Test 1

TOP TIME MANAGEMENT TIPS

- Read the whole passage and wordbank before answering the questions.
- Put in the words you know easily first of all.
- Try reading the words in the wordbank first, then the whole passage. This works well for some people.
- Cross out the words in the wordbank after you have inserted them in the passage.
- In tests with 15 words in the wordbank, only 10 of these words will be needed to complete the passage.

 ## INSTRUCTIONS

 You have 5 minutes to complete the following section.
You have 10 questions to complete within the time given.

Complete the passage by choosing the correct words from the wordbank. Write each answer as a capital letter in the spaces provided.

EXAMPLE

A jumper	**B** big	**C** write	**D** bone	**E** wall
F worn	**G** blue	**H** go	**I** try	**J** jumped

The cat ① J over the fence.

The correct answer is **J** *jumped*.

WORDBANK

A scrutinised	**B** discovered	**C** presence	**D** array	**E** entire
F survey	**G** studying	**H** visit	**I** scientists	**J** information

Boy Finds New Planet

Tom Wagg was 15 when he ① _____ a new planet. The school pupil from Newcastle-under-Lyme spotted the planet whilst on a work experience ② _____ to Keele University.

He found the planet by ③ _____ the ④ _____ received from the WASP project.

WASP stands for Wide Angle Search for Planets, which is an ⑤ _____ of lenses on robotic telescopes that ⑥ _____ the ⑦ _____ sky, and the data is then ⑧ _____ by ⑨ _____ across the world.

Tom noticed a dip in the data, which showed the ⑩ _____ of a planet.

Cloze Wordbank Test 2

 You have 5 minutes to complete the following section.
You have 10 questions to complete within the time given.

Complete the passage below by choosing the correct words from the wordbank. Write each answer as a capital letter in the spaces provided.

WORDBANK

A entirety	**B** symbolises	**C** god	**D** reveal	**E** carved
F terrain	**G** mythology	**H** bedrock	**I** awe	**J** shifting

The Great Sphinx of Giza

The Sphinx is ①............... from the ②............... of the Giza plateau and is an amazing and

mysterious sight.

The body of a lion with the head of a king or ③..............., it ④............... the wisdom, skills and

⑤............... of the ancient Egyptians.

Because of the changing desert ⑥..............., the Sphinx has been buried several times by the

⑦............... sands. In 1905, the sand had to be removed to ⑧............... the ⑨............... of this

magnificent 45-metre long, ⑩...............-inspiring statue.

DID YOU KNOW? *A Sphinx is a Greek mythological figure that set a riddle for passers-by: 'What walks on four legs in the morning, two at noon and three in the evening?' It devoured those who answered wrongly!*

Cloze Wordbank Test 3

Complete the passage below by choosing the correct words from the wordbank. Write each answer as a capital letter in the spaces provided.

WORDBANK

A safety	**B** buttonhole	**C** courageous	**D** marvel	**E** impending
F address	**G** procedure	**H** raids	**I** precious	**J** ensuring

Escape to the Country

Mother had a brown tie-on luggage label in her hand with my name and ① .... written on in

block capitals on one side. I remember staring into her gently smiling face as she carefully fastened

it through my ② .... She repeated the same ③ .... on my older brother Trevor.

When I look back on that day, I ④ .... at how ⑤ .... and selfless my mother was.

Thinking only of ⑥ .... the safety of her two most ⑦ .... people, she sent us away

from London, from the bombing ⑧ .... and constant fear of ⑨ .... danger, away to the

⑩ .... of the Cornish countryside.

Cloze Wordbank Test 4

 You have 5 minutes to complete the following section.
You have 10 questions to complete within the time given.

Complete the passage below by choosing the correct words from the wordbank. Write each answer as a capital letter in the spaces provided.

WORDBANK

A detector	**B** cascading	**C** protruding	**D** fingernail	**E** anticipation
F object	**G** quickening	**H** metal	**I** trowel	**J** crumbly

Treasure

Bobby's metal ① _____ went crazy with whines and whistles. Bobby knew he had found

something made of ② _____ in the ③ _____ soil beneath his feet.

Was it rubbish or was it treasure? With great ④ _____ and a ⑤ _____ heartbeat, he knelt

down and with his ⑥ _____, began to dig through the brown earth.

He nearly missed the small dark copper disc, no bigger than a ⑦ _____ , ⑧ _____ from the

trowel full of soil.

Bobby rubbed the dirt off the ⑨ _____ and saw that it was a coin of some sort.

Bending down, he dug again and lifted out a great brown clod of earth with many of the copper

discs ⑩ _____ from all sides.

NOW TRY THIS... *Write a story about treasure-seekers. Make sure you use a wide variety of adjectives to build description.*

Cloze Wordbank Test 5

Complete the passage below by choosing the correct words from the wordbank. Write each answer as a capital letter in the spaces provided.

WORDBANK

A disbelieving	**B** depicted	**C** fairies	**D** upon	**E** behind
F forbidden	**G** camera	**H** understandably	**I** demanded	**J** fascinating

Fairies

It was 1917 and Elsie Wright and her 10-year-old cousin Frances liked to go and play down by the

stream which ran through the fields ① .... Elsie's house.

However, they had been ② .... to go and ③ .... finding that they had spent the morning

there, her parents ④ .... to know what was so ⑤ .... about the place.

Elsie and Frances replied that they went to see the ⑥ ....

⑦ .... their parents were surprised and somewhat ⑧ ...., so the girls borrowed Elsie's

father's ⑨ .... and took it down to the stream to photograph the fairies. Indeed the first

photograph clearly ⑩ .... Frances with five small fairies dancing in front of her.

Cloze Wordbank Test 6

Complete the passage below by choosing the correct words from the wordbank. Write each answer as a capital letter in the spaces provided.

WORDBANK

A centre	**B** leading	**C** attempt	**D** believing	**E** record
F extremely	**G** disintegrate	**H** powered	**I** heavy	**J** current
K beast	**L** thankfully	**M** designed	**N** break	**O** dessert

The Bloodhound SSC

The Bloodhound SSC is a superfast car ① .... by a jet engine normally used in the Typhoon Eurofighter plane.

The world's ② .... engineers have ③ .... the Bloodhound to attempt to ④ .... the land speed ⑤ .... at salt flats in Hakskeen Pan, South Africa.

The team behind the ⑥ .... hope the car will reach speeds of 1000 mph, which would break the ⑦ .... world record of 783 mph.

Because of the high speeds reached, the wheels of the Bloodhound have to be ⑧ .... strong yet lightweight so that they will not ⑨ .... at such high speeds, yet not be so ⑩ .... that they slow the car down.

DID YOU KNOW? *To set the record, the Bloodhound will have to complete the course twice, in opposite directions. This prevents the wind helping the car travel faster.*

Cloze Wordbank Test 7

 You have 3 minutes to complete the following section.
You have 10 questions to complete within the time given.

Complete the passage below by choosing the correct words from the wordbank. Write each answer as a capital letter in the spaces provided.

WORDBANK

A frenzy	**B** early	**C** protecting	**D** structures	**E** permanent
F continued	**G** wood	**H** victory	**I** kingdom	**J** built

Castles

The first castles were ①............... by the Normans and this began the great age of castles, which

lasted for nearly 500 years.

The Normans constructed their first castles from ②............... . These were built after their

③............... at the Battle of Hastings in 1066. They needed a way of ④............... their new

⑤............... and so castles were built all over the land.

As this ⑥............... of castle building ⑦..............., the Normans began to build stone ⑧............... as

these were much stronger and therefore more ⑨............... . Many of these ⑩............... stone castles

are still standing today.

Cloze Wordbank Test 8

 You have 5 minutes to complete the following section.
You have 10 questions to complete within the time given.

Complete the passage below by choosing the correct words from the wordbank. Write each answer as a capital letter in the spaces provided.

WORDBANK

A butterflies	**B** migration	**C** second	**D** travelling	**E** northerly
F journey	**G** climates	**H** habitat	**I** patterned	**J** distinctive

Monarchs

The Monarch is one of the world's most famous ①............... . It has ②............... yellow and black

③............... wings and lives in the United States, Canada and Mexico.

It is well known because it makes an annual ④............... from ⑤............... areas such as Canada

to warmer ⑥............... in Mexico, sometimes ⑦............... 265 miles per day to cover the 3000-mile

⑧............... .

The Monarchs of Eastern North America have a ⑨............... home in the Sierra Madre Mountains

of Mexico, and this area is now a World Heritage Site in order to protect the overwintering

⑩............... of the Monarch.

NOW TRY THIS... *Research the Monarch butterfly and other insects. Write a formal report on your findings.*

Cloze Wordbank Test 9

Complete the passage below by choosing the correct words from the wordbank. Write each answer as a capital letter in the spaces provided.

WORDBANK

A accomplices	B nicknamed	C disguised	D ceremonial	E toughened
F apprehended	G acquired	H perpetrators	I Queen	J guarded

The Crown Jewels

Housed in the Tower of London, these ① .... treasures have been ② .... by the Kings and

Queens of England since 1660.

The Crown Jewels are part of the national heritage and held by the ③ .... as sovereign.

These precious items are on show to the public but are protected by ④ .... glass cabinets and

⑤ .... by the Yeoman Warders who are ⑥ .... Beefeaters.

On 9 May 1671, Thomas Blood was captured whilst trying to steal the Crown Jewels.

⑦ .... as a priest, Blood and three ⑧ .... fooled the guard and forced their way into the

Jewel House. However, the Tower guards ⑨ .... all four ⑩ ....

DID YOU KNOW? *According to legend, there must be six ravens in the Tower of London at all times or the kingdom and the Tower will both fall.*

Cloze Wordbank Test 10

 You have 5 minutes to complete the following section.
You have 10 questions to complete within the time given.

Complete the passage below by choosing the correct words from the wordbank. Write each answer as a capital letter in the spaces provided.

WORDBANK

| **A** average | **B** huddle | **C** feathers | **D** conditions | **E** groups |
| **F** protect | **G** fierce | **H** frigid | **I** flightless | **J** insulating |

Emperors

Emperors are the largest of all penguins and an ① .... bird stands around 115 centimetres tall, which is about the size of a six-year-old child.

These ② .... birds live on the Antarctic ice and in the ③ .... surrounding waters.

They survive – breeding, raising young and eating – because they have a large store of ④ .... body fat and several layers of scale-like ⑤ .... which ⑥ .... them from the ⑦ ...., icy winds.

The temperature can drop to minus 60 degrees centigrade and in these harsh ⑧ .... they will ⑨ .... close together in large ⑩ .... to keep themselves warm.

Cloze Wordbank Test 11

Complete the passage below by choosing the correct words from the wordbank. Write each answer as a capital letter in the spaces provided.

WORDBANK

A imprisoned	B inhabitants	C human	D knowledge	E memory
F divided	G subject	H useful	I arrived	J inhabited

The Tempest

The only ① .... of a certain island in the sea were a man named Prospero and his beautiful

daughter Miranda.

Miranda had ② .... on the island at such a young age that she had no ③ .... of having

seen any ④ .... face other than that of her father.

They lived in a cave ⑤ .... into rooms, one of which was Prospero's study where he kept all

his books on the ⑥ .... of magic.

His ⑦ .... of magic was very ⑧ .... on this island as it had been previously ⑨ ....

by a witch called Sycorax who, before she died, had ⑩ .... many good spirits in the trunks

of large trees.

DID YOU KNOW? *The Tempest is a play by William Shakespeare written around 1610–11. A tempest is a huge storm (which takes place in the first scene of the play). The island the play takes place on is probably a mixture of Bermuda and the Mediterranean.*

Cloze Wordbank Test 12

Complete the passage below by choosing the correct words from the wordbank. Write each answer as a capital letter in the spaces provided.

WORDBANK

A accompaniments	B sprig	C douse	D hearty	E traditional
F households	G offer	H mixture	I alight	J dessert

The Christmas Pudding

Christmas puddings are a ①............ Christmas ②............ typically eaten after the Christmas turkey and its ③............ .

In some ④............ the tradition is that the pudding should have a ⑤............ of holly on the top. The meaning behind this decoration was to ⑥............ protection over the family for the New Year.

Some families ⑦............ the pudding in brandy and set it ⑧............ before bringing it to the table to a ⑨............ round of applause.

It used to be the case that during the making of the Christmas pudding, a few coins would be placed in the ⑩............ and after it was baked and served, some lucky person would find the money in their portion.

Cloze Wordbank Test 13

 You have 4 minutes to complete the following section.
You have 10 questions to complete within the time given.

Complete the passage below by choosing the correct words from the wordbank. Write each answer as a capital letter in the spaces provided.

WORDBANK

A credited	**B** legend	**C** sacrifice	**D** hermit	**E** represent
F maiden	**G** demanded	**H** commonly	**I** living	**J** travels

St George and the Dragon

In the Middle Ages the dragon was ①_____ used to ②_____ the devil. The slaying of the

dragon by St George was first ③_____ to him in the twelfth century.

The ④_____ of St George and the dragon tells of St George's ⑤_____ through a country

called Libya, where he met a poor ⑥_____ who told him that everyone in this land was

⑦_____ in fear of a mighty dragon.

This dragon had ⑧_____ the ⑨_____ of every beautiful ⑩_____ in the land and now only

the King of Egypt's daughter was left alive.

DID YOU KNOW? A hagiography is the biography of a saint.

Cloze Wordbank Test 14

 You have 3 minutes to complete the following section.
You have 10 questions to complete within the time given.

Complete the passage below by choosing the correct words from the wordbank. Write each answer as a capital letter in the spaces provided.

WORDBANK

A created	**B** expert	**C** resembled	**D** talents	**E** machines
F particularly	**G** anatomy	**H** observations	**I** painter	**J** detailed

Leonardo da Vinci 1452–1519

Leonardo da Vinci wasn't just an incredible ①............: he was an inventor, scientist,

mathematician, engineer, writer, musician and much more.

He was a genius and his many ②............ and amazing inventions showed him to be a great thinker.

Leonardo was ③............ interested in flight and he ④............ plans for flying ⑤............ that

⑥............ the gliders and helicopters we see today.

He became an ⑦............ in the ⑧............ of the human body and produced hundreds of

⑨............ drawings from his ⑩............ .

DID YOU KNOW? *Leonardo da Vinci was a polymath. This means 'someone who has learned much' and who is talented in many different areas.*

Cloze Wordbank Test 15

 You have 5 minutes to complete the following section.
You have 10 questions to complete within the time given.

Complete the passage below by choosing the correct words from the wordbank. Write each answer as a capital letter in the spaces provided.

WORDBANK

A pleasure	**B** Norway	**C** weakness	**D** woodland	**E** longships
F coasts	**G** evidence	**H** adventurers	**I** North	**J** plunder
K exists	**L** fashion	**M** common	**N** terrific	**O** emergency

Vikings

In the time of the Vikings, warriors aboard their ①_____ travelled across the seas to loot,

②_____ and conquer.

They were great ③_____ and were always looking for new places to raid.

The Vikings came from ④_____, which lies across the ⑤_____ Sea from the east

⑥_____ of England and Scotland.

⑦_____ of their conquests still ⑧_____ today and can be found in many of the names

of towns and villages, particularly in the county of Yorkshire.

Place names with 'thorpe' or 'thwaite' are ⑨_____ in Yorkshire and these words mean

settlement and ⑩_____ clearing. This is a clear indication that these were originally

Viking villages.

Cloze Wordbank Test 16

 You have 3 minutes to complete the following section.
You have 10 questions to complete within the time given.

Complete the passage below by choosing the correct words from the wordbank. Write each answer as a capital letter in the spaces provided.

WORDBANK

A unlike	B dimensional	C piece	D three	E bounces
F pictures	G captures	H object	I light	J depth

Holograms

Holography is ①............... any other way of making ②................. Holograms are ③...............-

dimensional whereas a photograph is two- ④...............

The two dimensions of a photograph are width and height, but the hologram also has ⑤...............

Holograms are made by bouncing light off an ⑥............... . When the wave of ⑦............... hits the

object, it takes on the shape of that object. Once this shape has been made, it ⑧............... off onto

a ⑨............... of photographic film, which ⑩............... these light images.

DID YOU KNOW? *Salvador Dali claimed he was the first Surrealist artist to use holograms in art exhibitions.*

Cloze Wordbank Test 17

 You have 3 minutes to complete the following section.
You have 10 questions to complete within the time given.

Complete the passage below by choosing the correct words from the wordbank. Write each answer as a capital letter in the spaces provided.

WORDBANK

A spotted	**B** browsing	**C** name	**D** eagerly	**E** visited
F bought	**G** upon	**H** second	**I** author	**J** much

Coincidence

In the 1920s an American ①_____, called Anne Parrish, ②_____ Paris with her husband.

Whilst ③_____ in a ④_____-hand bookshop in the city, she found a book she had loved

reading as a child. It was called *Jack Frost and Other Stories*.

She ⑤_____ the book and ⑥_____ showed it to her husband, telling him how ⑦_____ she

had enjoyed reading it when she was a little girl.

⑧_____ opening the book her husband ⑨_____ a ⑩_____ written on the inside page

which read: 'Anne Parrish, 209 N. Weber Street, Colorado Springs'.

It was her book!

NOW TRY THIS... *Write a mystery story about coincidences. Ensure you develop a truly mysterious character!*

Cloze Wordbank Test 18

 You have 4 minutes to complete the following section.
You have 10 questions to complete within the time given.

Complete the passage below by choosing the correct words from the wordbank. Write each answer as a capital letter in the spaces provided.

WORDBANK

A launched	**B** turn	**C** donations	**D** debt	**E** partake
F match	**G** famous	**H** afternoon	**I** exercise	**J** saved

Manchester United

Manchester United, the world's most ① .... football club, was ② .... in 1878 by a band

of railway workers who wanted to ③ .... in some Saturday ④ .... physical ⑤ ....

The club flourished for the next thirty years but by the ⑥ .... of the century was in ⑦ ....

and in danger of winding up.

It was in fact a St Bernard dog named Major who ⑧ .... the club.

Harry Stafford, the club's skipper, used his pet dog Major as an attraction and on ⑨ .... days

he would send his dog into the crowd to collect ⑩ .... of money.

Cloze Wordbank Test 19

 You have 4 minutes to complete the following section.
You have 10 questions to complete within the time given.

Complete the passage below by choosing the correct words from the wordbank. Write each answer as a capital letter in the spaces provided.

WORDBANK

A typically	B rechargeable	C device	D popularity	E pressure
F arranged	G positions	H popular	I developed	J attributed

Hoverboards

Hoverboards are self-balancing, two-wheeled electric skateboards. They are powered by

① .... batteries and are easily portable.

The hoverboard is ② .... a plastic platform set on two wheels. The wheels are ③ ....

side by side; over these the rider ④ .... their feet.

The ⑤ .... is controlled by applying ⑥ .... with the feet on the built-in gyroscopic,

sensored pads.

The hoverboard was first ⑦ .... in China and quickly became ⑧ .... in many parts of the

world. The increase in ⑨ .... has been ⑩ .... to the many celebrities who have been seen

with these devices.

Cloze Wordbank Test 20

 You have 4 minutes to complete the following section.
You have 10 questions to complete within the time given.

Complete the passage below by choosing the correct words from the wordbank. Write each answer as a capital letter in the spaces provided.

WORDBANK

A gold	B bodies	C metals	D million	E travels
F digesting	G growing	H exercise	I muscles	J knowledge

The Human Body

All the time your body is carrying out a ① .... or more processes that you are completely

unaware of. You may be ② .... your breakfast, carrying oxygen around your body and

③ .... new skin and bones without your ④ ....

Our bodies make up to six cups of saliva a day and your blood ⑤ .... 12 000 miles around

your body in one day!

When your teacher says you are 'as good as gold', well you really are, as 0.2 mg of ⑥ .... is

in your body, most of it in the blood. However, it would take the blood of 40 000 people to make

an 8 g coin. We also have other ⑦ .... in our bodies such as zinc, copper and nickel.

Another surprising fact about our ⑧ .... is that when we smile we ⑨ .... about 36

different ⑩ ....

NOW TRY THIS... *Research some other idioms as well as 'good as gold'. How many can you find and what do they mean?*

Cloze Wordbank Test 21

 You have 4 minutes to complete the following section.
You have 10 questions to complete within the time given.

Complete the passage below by choosing the correct words from the wordbank. Write each answer as a capital letter in the spaces provided.

WORDBANK

A cut	B consisting	C roll	D spread	E pre-cooked
F arrange	G process	H served	I require	J firmly

Sushi

Sushi is a Japanese dish ①.............. of small rolls of cold rice, vegetables, tropical foods and raw

seafood. It is usually ②.............. with soy sauce or wasabi.

To make your own sushi you will need to do the following:

Place one nori sheet shiny side down on a sushi mat and spread three quarters of a cup of

③.............. rice over the nori.

Now ④.............. two teaspoons of mayonnaise over the centre of the rice.

⑤.............. about one quarter of a cucumber, some avocado and carrot over the mayonnaise

and then, using the sushi mat, ⑥.............. up ⑦.............. .

⑧.............. the long roll into six smaller slices and repeat the ⑨.............. to achieve the number

of pieces of sushi you ⑩.............. .

Cloze Wordbank Test 22

 You have 4 minutes to complete the following section.
You have 10 questions to complete within the time given.

Complete the passage below by choosing the correct words from the wordbank. Write each answer as a capital letter in the spaces provided.

WORDBANK

A bedrooms	**B** instead	**C** temporary	**D** deer	**E** sleeping
F reconstructed	**G** experience	**H** year	**I** temperatures	**J** visitors

Ice Hotel

An ice hotel is a ①............ hotel made of snow and sculpted blocks of ice. These hotels melt away

in the spring and have to be ②............ every ③............ .

Hotels made of ice can only be built in places which ④............ sub-zero ⑤............ during the

months from November to March. Places such as Finland and Canada have ice hotels.

⑥............ to the ice hotels sleep in ⑦............ where the beds are made of ice blocks but covered

with mattresses and ⑧............ furs and topped with Arctic ⑨............ bags.

Ice hotels have restaurants and bars but ⑩............ of swimming pools there are hot tubs

and saunas.

DID YOU KNOW? *The first ice hotel was opened in Quebec in 2001.*

Cloze Wordbank Test 23

Complete the passage below by choosing the correct words from the wordbank. Write each answer as a capital letter in the spaces provided.

WORDBANK

A dense	**B** tortoise	**C** escape	**D** briefly	**E** divine
F captors	**G** survive	**H** pollute	**I** captured	**J** describe
K managed	**L** regal	**M** aloof	**N** adrift	**O** rescued

Castaways

A castaway is a person who is cast ①............ on a boat or cast ashore on land.

Many stories about castaways ②............ how they managed to ③............ and are eventually rescued from their predicament.

One such person was Philip Ashton. Born in America in 1702, he was ④............ by pirates whilst fishing near the coast.

He managed to ⑤............ from his ⑥............ when the pirate ship landed ⑦............ on a small island in South America. Philip hid in the ⑧............ jungle until the pirates eventually left.

He ⑨............ to survive for 16 months until he was ⑩............ by a passing ship.

NOW TRY THIS... *Write a Haiku about being shipwrecked. Research Haikus if you have never written one before.*

Cloze Wordbank Test 24

 You have 5 minutes to complete the following section.
You have 10 questions to complete within the time given.

Complete the passage below by choosing the correct words from the wordbank. Write each answer as a capital letter in the spaces provided.

WORDBANK

A surname	**B** information	**C** hereditary	**D** introduce	**E** identified
F passed	**G** necessary	**H** communities	**I** original	**J** adopted

Surnames in England

Before 1066, people did not have surnames because ① .... were small and each person was

easily ② .... by a single name.

As the years passed and towns and cities grew much bigger, it gradually became ③ .... to

add more ④ .... to the ⑤ .... name. This gave rise to names such as John the weaver,

Mary from the wood, Robert son of Harry. Over time this extra information became the

⑥ ....; for example, John Weaver, Mary Wood and Robert Harrison.

After 1066, the Norman barons began to ⑦ .... a second name and these began to be

⑧ .... on to the next generation. By 1400 most English families had ⑨ .... the use of

⑩ .... surnames.

Cloze Wordbank Test 25

 You have 4 minutes to complete the following section.
You have 10 questions to complete within the time given.

Complete the passage below by choosing the correct words from the wordbank. Write each answer as a capital letter in the spaces provided.

WORDBANK

A raised	B listening	C represented	D accident	E frustrating
F signs	G attended	H invented	I fingertips	J code

Louis Braille

Louis Braille ①............ a way for blind people to read books.

He became blind at the age of three following an ②............ in his father's workshop. He

③............ a school for blind children but found it very ④............ that he had to learn everything

by just ⑤............ .

When he was 12 years old, he invented a ⑥............ of six ⑦............ dots that ⑧............ words

and letters. The blind person could read these words by running their ⑨............ over the

raised dots.

Now practically every country uses Braille and it is also used on food labelling and medicine

packaging and on ⑩............ in public places.

DID YOU KNOW? *Louis Braille even created symbols for maths and music.*

Cloze Wordbank Test 26

Complete the passage below by choosing the correct words from the wordbank. Write each answer as a capital letter in the spaces provided.

WORDBANK

A marker	**B** carefully	**C** person	**D** featured	**E** people
F typically	**G** region	**H** landmarks	**I** Canada	**J** stretched

Inukshuks

An inukshuk is a man-made stone landmark used by the ①............... of the Arctic ②............... of

North America. The inukshuk acted as a navigation ③............... for travel routes, fishing places,

camps, hunting grounds and many other ④............... .

These landmarks ⑤............... stand about two to three metres high and look rather like a

⑥............... standing with their arms ⑦............... out.

These inukshuks are made from stones piled up ⑧............... on top of one another. The tallest

one was built in ⑨............... and was 11 metres tall and ⑩............... in the Guinness Book of

World Records.

DID YOU KNOW? *In Inuit language, Inukshuk means 'in the likeness of a human'.*

Cloze Wordbank Test 27

 You have 5 minutes to complete the following section.
You have 10 questions to complete within the time given.

Complete the passage below by choosing the correct words from the wordbank. Write each answer as a capital letter in the spaces provided.

WORDBANK

A lotus	**B** indicate	**C** celebration	**D** goddess	**E** believed
F drawn	**G** homes	**H** design	**I** symbols	**J** infinity

Diwali

During Diwali, the Hindu festival of light, the ①_____ Lakshmi is ②_____ to visit homes that

are bright and well lit. Families light many candles and decorate their ③_____ with rangoli

designs.

A rangoli ④_____ is created on the doorstep to welcome visitors who are arriving to join the

⑤_____. Motifs used in the pattern are celestial ⑥_____ of light such as the sun and the

moon, along with circular and spiral lines to depict ⑦_____ or time never ending.

The ⑧_____ flower is also ⑨_____ with 24 petals and goddess Lakshmi's footprints are

painted near the door with the toes facing inside to ⑩_____ her arrival.

Cloze Wordbank Test 28

 You have 4 minutes to complete the following section.
You have 10 questions to complete within the time given.

Complete the passage below by choosing the correct words from the wordbank. Write each answer as a capital letter in the spaces provided.

WORDBANK

A single	B risk	C environment	D need	E challenges
F receives	G examples	H tirelessly	I recognition	J volunteer

Unsung Heroes

Someone who does a great job but ① .... little or no ② .... for what they do can be

described as an unsung hero.

They may help people in ③ ...., perhaps ④ .... their lives for the safety of others, or

work ⑤ .... to improve the lives of animals or help the ⑥ ....

They do these things without expecting any reward even though they may have faced huge

⑦ .... themselves.

Some ⑧ .... of unsung heroes might be those people who treat the homeless as their

brothers and sisters, those who ⑨ .... to work for charities, or parents who bring up families

⑩ ....-handedly.

Cloze Wordbank Test 29

 You have 5 minutes to complete the following section.
You have 10 questions to complete within the time given.

Complete the passage below by choosing the correct words from the wordbank. Write each answer as a capital letter in the spaces provided.

WORDBANK

A activities	B body	C energetic	D requires	E popular
F hundreds	G unusual	H thread	I satisfaction	J manipulate

Hobbies

Having a hobby is very important for everyone. It brings pleasure, enjoyment and ①................ .

There are ②................ of different hobbies from astronomy or archery to birdwatching or bicycling.

Some hobbies are more ③................ than others. Cheerleading includes moving every part of

your ④................ whereas cross-stitch only ⑤................ your fingers to ⑥................ the needle and

⑦................ .

⑧................ hobbies are dancing, football, horse riding or Lego construction and most of us take

part in these ⑨................ at some point. More ⑩................ hobbies might be matchstick modelling,

shark fishing or wrestling.

NOW TRY THIS... *Find out from your friends about their hobbies. Which is the most unusual?*

Cloze Wordbank Test 30

 You have 3 minutes to complete the following section.
You have 10 questions to complete within the time given.

Complete the passage below by choosing the correct words from the wordbank. Write each answer as a capital letter in the spaces provided.

WORDBANK

A contents	B bones	C within	D identified	E number
F undigested	G hunting	H produce	I period	J vegetable

Owl Pellets

Owls and most other birds ①............ pellets. Pellets are small sausage-shaped lumps of

②............ parts of the birds' food, which are ejected through the mouth.

Owl pellets are easy to find and study. They do not pass through the owl's intestines and do not

smell and therefore are not unpleasant to work with.

The pellets are easily broken apart and contain tiny ③............ of small mammals and birds

eaten by the owl, which can be seen ④............ this parcel of matter along with fur, feathers and

⑤............ fibre.

Once the ⑥............ of the pellet have been ⑦............, it is possible to find out where the owl has

been ⑧............ and the ⑨............ of animals it has eaten over a 24-hour ⑩............ .

DID YOU KNOW? *It takes an owl six hours or more to regurgitate a pellet after eating.*

Cloze Wordbank Test 31

 You have 3 minutes to complete the following section.
You have 10 questions to complete within the time given.

Complete the passage below by choosing the correct words from the wordbank. Write each answer as a capital letter in the spaces provided.

WORDBANK

A brave	**B** villagers	**C** north	**D** floral	**E** outside
F death	**G** creation	**H** plague	**I** disease	**J** embroidery
K magnified	**L** parcel	**M** carried	**N** bounding	**O** decision

The Village of Eyam and the Plague

In the summer of 1665, the tailor in the small Derbyshire village of Eyam received a ① .... of

cloth from London.

This cloth had fleas in it which ② .... bubonic ③ .... Within a week the tailor was dead

from the plague and soon another five villagers also died.

The ④ .... quickly made a very heroic ⑤ .... To prevent the ⑥ .... from spreading

to the other towns and villages in the ⑦ .... of England, they decided to cut themselves off

from the ⑧ .... world even though this could mean ⑨ .... for perhaps all of them.

People who lived outside the village heard about the ⑩ .... decision they had made and

supplied them with food which was left at the edge of the village for the heroic villagers to pick up.

NOW TRY THIS... *Imagine how you would have felt as a villager in Eyam. Write a description of your thoughts and feelings.*

Cloze Wordbank Test 32

 You have 4 minutes to complete the following section.
You have 10 questions to complete within the time given.

Complete the passage below by choosing the correct words from the wordbank. Write each answer as a capital letter in the spaces provided.

WORDBANK

A bulging	**B** replenished	**C** lessen	**D** pencil	**E** blazer
F smell	**G** brown	**H** adjusted	**I** ink	**J** stature

Satchels

The day had arrived. I checked my pockets carefully. Yes, there was the bus pass in its shiny plastic cover lying in my ① .... pocket.

My ② .... leather satchel with my initials stamped on the front was by the back door with the leather strap ③ .... for my small ④ .... Satchels were made to last until you left school, which was most probably seven years.

The ⑤ .... of leather was everywhere in the new school. I remember that it never seemed to ⑥ ...., always ⑦ .... with the next intake of first years – satchels everywhere ⑧ .... with books and ⑨ .... cases.

It was easy to tell the satchels of older pupils as they were nearly all covered with writing – usually the names of pop stars, boyfriends or football teams – the once smooth, conker-brown satchels now tattooed with blue and black ⑩ ....

Cloze Wordbank Test 33

You have 4 minutes to complete the following section.
You have 10 questions to complete within the time given.

Complete the passage below by choosing the correct words from the wordbank. Write each answer as a capital letter in the spaces provided.

WORDBANK

A suspended	**B** mainland	**C** passengers	**D** steps	**E** exposes
F avoiding	**G** causeway	**H** separating	**I** obstructions	**J** turns

The Sea Tractor

When the tide is in, ① .... the island from the mainland, the giant sea tractor takes the

passengers through the waves to the island's hotel.

The sea tractor is really a monster tractor. It has a platform ② .... about two metres above

the chassis. The passengers climb up metal ③ .... onto a platform with wooden sides.

The sea tractor travels through the waves, carefully ④ .... any underwater ⑤ .... such

as large rocks, and drives up to the concrete landing. The ⑥ .... disembark onto the island.

The sea tractor picks up passengers returning to the ⑦ .... and repeats this journey until the

tide ⑧ .... and ⑨ .... the sandy ⑩ .... once more.

Cloze Wordbank Test 34

 You have 3 minutes to complete the following section.
You have 10 questions to complete within the time given.

Complete the passage below by choosing the correct words from the wordbank. Write each answer as a capital letter in the spaces provided.

WORDBANK

A myth	**B** Monster	**C** reputedly	**D** lake	**E** appreciating
F deepest	**G** attracts	**H** loch	**I** conclusive	**J** scenery

Loch Ness

① .... is the Scottish Gaelic word for a lake or sea inlet. Loch Ness is a Scottish

② .... 23 miles long and at its ③ .... point is 230 metres below the surface.

It is very beautiful and ④ .... many visitors who, besides ⑤ .... the ⑥ ....,

look hopefully across the loch for the Loch Ness ⑦ ....

The Loch Ness Monster, known as Nessie, has ⑧ .... been seen by many people, but the

evidence for its existence is not ⑨ .... and therefore the story is regarded by non-believers

as a modern ⑩ ....

DID YOU KNOW? *Cryptozoology is the science of animals that have not been proven to exist, although people claim to have seen them.*

Cloze Wordbank Test 35

 You have 4 minutes to complete the following section.
You have 10 questions to complete within the time given.

Complete the passage below by choosing the correct words from the wordbank. Write each answer as a capital letter in the spaces provided.

WORDBANK

A months	**B** chopped	**C** celebrate	**D** worshipping	**E** fragrant
F preach	**G** evergreen	**H** origins	**I** believed	**J** traditionally

Christmas Tree

For thousands of years the ①............. fir tree has been used to ②............. winter festivals. The

③............. green branches made people think of spring and cheered them up during the dark,

cold winter ④.............

It is ⑤............. that fir trees were first used as Christmas trees in northern Europe and were

⑥............. hung upside down.

One story about the ⑦............. of Christmas trees comes from England. St Boniface of Crediton,

Devon travelled to Germany to ⑧............. about Christianity when he came upon some people

⑨............. an oak tree. This annoyed St Boniface so much that he ⑩............. the oak tree down

and he was amazed to see a young fir tree spring up in its place. He then hung the fir tree with

candles so he could continue preaching when darkness fell.

NOW TRY THIS... *Write a vivid description of a Christmas tree. What makes it so captivating?*

Cloze Wordbank Test 36

 You have 4 minutes to complete the following section.
You have 10 questions to complete within the time given.

Complete the passage below by choosing the correct words from the wordbank. Write each answer as a capital letter in the spaces provided.

WORDBANK

A villain	**B** festival	**C** traced	**D** fairy	**E** characters
F theme	**G** plot	**H** century	**I** reflect	**J** opposite

Pantomime

Pantomimes first came to Britain in the thirteenth ① .... from Italy.

The plays usually had ② .... such as clowns, a jester and a ③ .... The ④ .... was

often mixed up with traditional ⑤ .... tales.

The earliest pantomimes can be ⑥ .... back to the ancient Roman midwinter festival of

'Saturnalia'. The ⑦ .... of this ⑧ .... was that everything in nature was upside down.

Winter was the ⑨ .... of summer; the days were darker and in summer they were lighter. To

⑩ .... this idea, the male characters in the Roman plays were women dressed as men and the

men dressed as women, which is more or less what happens in our modern-day pantomimes.

Cloze Wordbank Test 37

Complete the passage below by choosing the correct words from the wordbank. Write each answer as a capital letter in the spaces provided.

WORDBANK

A stimulation	B highly	C requires	D owner	E energetic
F breed	G referred	H physical	I shepherds	J mainly

Border Collie

The Border Collie is often ① .... to as a sheepdog, ② .... because this type of dog is a

working and herding ③ .... and is used primarily to herd sheep.

Border Collies are ④ .... intelligent, ⑤ .... and athletic. Besides being excellent

⑥ ...., they can compete in dog sports and agility demonstrations.

Because the Border Collie is highly intelligent, it ⑦ .... mental ⑧ .... as well as

⑨ .... exercise. Herding flocks of sheep fulfils both of these requirements. However, most

Border Collies are family pets and if this is the case, the ⑩ .... will need to actively play with

their pets using balls, Frisbees and chew toys.

Cloze Wordbank Test 38

 You have 3 minutes to complete the following section.
You have 10 questions to complete within the time given.

Complete the passage below by choosing the correct words from the wordbank. Write each answer as a capital letter in the spaces provided.

WORDBANK

A species	B puncture	C landing	D aware	E tongue
F wound	G infected	H spread	I prey	J diseases

Vampire Bats

In South America there is a ①_____ of bat that feeds solely on the blood of its ②_____. The vampire bat feeds on the blood of cattle and other animals by ③_____ on their bodies whilst they are asleep. They use their teeth to ④_____ the flesh and then they use their ⑤_____ to lick up the blood that flows out of the ⑥_____.

Because the skin of cattle is very thick, the animal will not be ⑦_____ of the bat or the wound and will continue to sleep.

The vampire bat can ⑧_____ diseases, including viruses that can make animals ill. These ⑨_____ can be spread to humans; therefore many farmers trap the bats as they don't want their livestock to be ⑩_____.

NOW TRY THIS... Write a report about vampire bats' habitats and include some interesting incidents involving them.

Cloze Wordbank Test 39

 You have 3 minutes to complete the following section.
You have 10 questions to complete within the time given.

Complete the passage below by choosing the correct words from the wordbank. Write each answer as a capital letter in the spaces provided.

WORDBANK

A played	**B** survived	**C** stolen	**D** advantage	**E** several
F silver	**G** era	**H** character	**I** original	**J** version

Ruby Slippers

In the Wizard of Oz a pair of magic shoes was worn by Dorothy Gale, the main ①............... in

the story.

In the famous film ②............... of the story, Dorothy was ③............... by an actress called Judy

Garland. There were in fact ④............... pairs of the shoes made and five pairs ⑤............... until

2005 when one pair was ⑥............... and has never been found.

In the ⑦............... novel, written in 1900, Dorothy wears ⑧............... shoes but these were changed

to red in the 1939 film in order to take full ⑨............... of the new ⑩............... of Technicolor film.

Cloze Wordbank Test 40

 You have 3 minutes to complete the following section.
You have 10 questions to complete within the time given.

Complete the passage below by choosing the correct words from the wordbank. Write each answer as a capital letter in the spaces provided.

WORDBANK

A avoid	**B** jams	**C** school	**D** hours	**E** ranked
F capital	**G** worst	**H** journey	**I** stranded	**J** reason

Traffic Jams

In Jakarta, Indonesia's ① _____ city, many children are in ② _____ sitting at their desks

by 6:30 a.m. The ③ _____ for this early start is to ④ _____ and lessen the terrible traffic

⑤ _____ which happen every morning and make what should be a 15-minute ⑥ _____ three

or four times longer.

Jakarta, Istanbul and Mexico City are ⑦ _____ amongst the world's ⑧ _____ cities for traffic

jams. It often happens in these cities that cars become gridlocked for ⑨ _____ at a time. This

means you can be ⑩ _____ in a jam and not move at all. Another of the worst places for traffic

is the African country of Uganda, where traffic jams are often at a standstill for hours and it has

been known to take 7 hours to travel 5 kilometres.

NOW TRY THIS... What would you do if you were stuck in traffic for seven hours? Write a paragraph explaining how you would pass the time. Be inventive!

Cloze Wordbank Test 41

Complete the passage below by choosing the correct words from the wordbank. Write each answer as a capital letter in the spaces provided.

WORDBANK

A Wednesday	B lessons	C students	D early	E water
F ends	G clean	H different	I chores	J leaving

School Days

In China a typical school day runs from 7:30 a.m. to 5 p.m. and summer holidays are mostly spent in summer classes so the holidays aren't holidays at all.

French children typically go to school from 8 a.m. to 4 p.m. and attend school on Saturday, though not on ①_____. They do, however, have a long summer holiday when schools close for July and August.

Children in Ghana often get up as ②_____ as 4 a.m. as they have to do ③_____ in the home, such as fetching ④_____ or sweeping, before setting off for school which usually starts at 7:30 a.m. School ⑤_____ at 2:15 p.m. but some students stay later to have private ⑥_____ with their teachers.

Things are very ⑦_____ again in South Korea where school days are from 8 a.m. to 4 p.m. but many ⑧_____ stay on to work much later and are expected to ⑨_____ their classrooms before ⑩_____.

Cloze Wordbank Test 42

 You have 4 minutes to complete the following section.
You have 10 questions to complete within the time given.

Complete the passage below by choosing the correct words from the wordbank. Write each answer as a capital letter in the spaces provided.

WORDBANK

A baby	**B** respectively	**C** gender	**D** given	**E** grown
F under	**G** animal	**H** categorised	**I** regardless	**J** between

Types of Horses

Types of horses are ① .... according to whether they are male or female, how old they are and how big they are.

A ② .... horse less than a year old is called a foal and a yearling is the name ③ .... to a young horse ④ .... the ages of one and two.

A colt is a male horse ⑤ .... four years old and a filly is the name for a female horse of the same age.

Fully- ⑥ .... male and female horses are called stallions and mares ⑦ ....

However, a pony is just a small horse and has that name ⑧ .... of the ⑨ .... or the age of the ⑩ ....

DID YOU KNOW? *To be called a pony, a horse has to be under 147 cm tall at the top of its withers (shoulders).*

Cloze Wordbank Test 43

 You have 3 minutes to complete the following section.
You have 10 questions to complete within the time given.

Complete the passage below by choosing the correct words from the wordbank. Write each answer as a capital letter in the spaces provided.

WORDBANK

A bumpy	**B** power	**C** hidden	**D** spacecraft	**E** Earth
F sunlight	**G** panels	**H** leaving	**I** transmit	**J** comet

Philae

The Philae Lander is the first ever ① .... to land on a comet.

In November 2014, after ② .... its mother ship, Rosetta, the Philae Lander landed on a

③ .... Unfortunately it was a ④ .... landing and the solar panels were ⑤ .... from

the sun.

The solar panels provided the Philae Lander with its ⑥ .... which therefore could not

⑦ .... any information back to ⑧ ....

Scientists hoped that some ⑨ .... would eventually reach the ⑩ .... and this proved to be

the case several months later.

DID YOU KNOW? *Philae is named after the Philae obelisk, which was used to interpret and translate Egyptian hieroglyphics.*

Cloze Wordbank Test 44

 You have 3 minutes to complete the following section.
You have 10 questions to complete within the time given.

Complete the passage below by choosing the correct words from the wordbank. Write each answer as a capital letter in the spaces provided.

WORDBANK

A sometimes	B combines	C climbing	D soccer	E involves
F venues	G giant	H country	I challenging	J variation

Zorbing

Zorbing is a sport which ① .... a person ② .... into a ③ .... transparent ball and

then, by making a running movement, moving the ball along.

This is very ④ .... to do on land and some people prefer to do it on water.

Zorbing is ⑤ .... called sphering or orbing and can be enjoyed at ⑥ .... all around

the ⑦ ....

Bubble ⑧ .... is a ⑨ .... of zorbing. It ⑩ .... zorbing and soccer and is a fun sport

for all ages.

Cloze Wordbank Test 45

 You have 5 minutes to complete the following section.
You have 10 questions to complete within the time given.

Complete the passage below by choosing the correct words from the wordbank. Write each answer as a capital letter in the spaces provided.

WORDBANK

A reflected	**B** admired	**C** baskets	**D** yearly	**E** carefully
F imagination	**G** poison	**H** shiny	**I** pond	**J** lazy
K capital	**L** flexible	**M** represent	**N** sprinkle	**O** picked

Miniature Gardens

My best friend and I made a teeny weeny garden using an old tea tray and our ① ....

We collected lots of springy green moss from the top of the stone wall. It was perfect for the little lawn area.

The tiny pebbles at the base of the wall were small enough to ② .... in between the moss to ③ .... the gravel path.

④ ...., we made tiny flowerbeds using soil and the mini flower heads ⑤ .... from the alyssum and lobelia growing in Mother's hanging ⑥ ....

Tiny fences were made from birch bark strips, and an archway curved over the entrance to the fairy garden.

Mother gave us an old handbag mirror for a ⑦ .... and we fashioned four-leaf clover into minute lily pads. We ⑧ .... how the little garden was ⑨ .... so beautifully in the mirror's ⑩ .... surface.

NOW TRY THIS... *Make a miniature garden using any suitable objects you can find.*

Cloze Wordbank Test 46

 You have 4 minutes to complete the following section.
You have 10 questions to complete within the time given.

Complete the passage below by choosing the correct words from the wordbank. Write each answer as a capital letter in the spaces provided.

WORDBANK

A colonised	B bred	C roam	D reports	E kangaroo
F pair	G loose	H advice	I colony	J incident

Wallabies

A wallaby is an animal which looks like a small ① .... and is usually found in Australia and

New Guinea. However, over the years wallabies have ② .... parts of the UK and are happily

living in the forests and fields of many counties. For example, a ③ .... of more than a hundred

wallabies can be found on the Isle of Man, having ④ .... originally from a ⑤ .... that

escaped from a wildlife park.

Police were called to an ⑥ .... in York involving ⑦ .... of a wallaby on the ⑧ .... on

the city's ring road. The ⑨ .... from the RSPCA was to leave it to ⑩ .... free after it had

been chased off the road and into the countryside.

Cloze Wordbank Test 47

 You have 5 minutes to complete the following section.
You have 10 questions to complete within the time given.

Complete the passage below by choosing the correct words from the wordbank. Write each answer as a capital letter in the spaces provided.

WORDBANK

A winter	**B** describe	**C** appropriate	**D** performing	**E** recreational
F developed	**G** inspired	**H** clothing	**I** techniques	**J** involves

Snowboarding

Snowboarding was ① .... by skateboarding and, besides being a ② .... activity, it is an

Olympic sport.

Since snowboarding began as an established ③ .... sport, many ④ .... and skills have

been ⑤ .... These skills have required new words to ⑥ .... the manoeuvres. Examples of

these are jibbing and freeriding.

Freestyle snowboarding ⑦ .... the rider ⑧ .... tricks using man-made or natural ramps.

Special ⑨ .... is required as wearing the ⑩ .... apparel enables the rider to move their

body easily in order to perform the moves and tricks.

Cloze Wordbank Test 48

 You have 4 minutes to complete the following section.
You have 10 questions to complete within the time given.

Complete the passage below by choosing the correct words from the wordbank. Write each answer as a capital letter in the spaces provided.

WORDBANK

A spike	**B** easy	**C** drip	**D** caves	**E** formations
F remember	**G** formed	**H** refers	**I** down	**J** commonly

Stalagmites and Stalactites

Stalagmites and stalactites are types of rock ① .... usually found in underground caverns.

A stalagmite rises from the floor of the cave like a ② .... of rock. It is ③ .... by the accumulation of minerals which ④ .... from the roof of the cave.

Stalactites hang ⑤ .... from the ceiling of the cave and are also made from mineral accumulations.

Stalagmites are most ⑥ .... found in limestone ⑦ .... such as Poole's Cavern in Derbyshire.

An ⑧ .... way to ⑨ .... which word ⑩ .... to which formation is that stalagmite has a 'g' for ground and stalactite has a 'c' for ceiling.

DID YOU KNOW? *Stalagmites and stalactites can form from many different substances, including ice, lava, limestone and cement.*

Cloze Wordbank Test 49

 You have 4 minutes to complete the following section.
You have 10 questions to complete within the time given.

Complete the passage below by choosing the correct words from the wordbank. Write each answer as a capital letter in the spaces provided.

WORDBANK

A swimmer	**B** rapidly	**C** surfaces	**D** towering	**E** participants
F inflatable	**G** tumbles	**H** allows	**I** physical	**J** riverbed

Rafting on the Colorado

To take a rafting trip down the Colorado River you need to be in good ① _____ condition and a

strong ② _____.

The current is fierce and the river ③ _____ and crashes over rocks on the ④ _____.

Beneath the ⑤ _____ walls of the Grand Canyon, you sit in an ⑥ _____ boat along with

several other people. With one paddle each, you attempt to direct the raft as it moves ⑦ _____

downstream.

The flexibility of the inflatable raft ⑧ _____ it to bend over the many rocks and uneven

⑨ _____.

It is easy to see how quickly the raft could tip over and why the ⑩ _____ need to be strong

swimmers.

NOW TRY THIS... *Write an account of an adventure for a magazine.*

Cloze Wordbank Test 50

 You have 4 minutes to complete the following section.
You have 10 questions to complete within the time given.

Complete the passage below by choosing the correct words from the wordbank. Write each answer as a capital letter in the spaces provided.

WORDBANK

A enjoy	B creative	C partner	D funky	E suits
F classical	G everyone	H dancing	I modern	J healthy

Dance

Dancing is a fantastic way to ① .... yourself and keep ② .... and fit at the same time.

There are many types of ③ .... and ④ .... can find the style which ⑤ .... them best.

Ballet is a ⑥ .... dance and the dancers move to classical music, whereas jazz dance has a

very loose and free style and the music is very ⑦ .... and upbeat.

Ballroom dancing involves dancing with a ⑧ .... and hip-hop is a newcomer to the dance

scene, in which the dancers move in a very ⑨ .... way to modern, ⑩ .... music.

Cloze Wordbank Test 51

Complete the passage below by choosing the correct words from the wordbank. Write each answer as a capital letter in the spaces provided.

WORDBANK

A workers	B reference	C filling	D throughout	E Cornwall
F case	G convenient	H century	I diet	J crusts

The Cornish Pasty

The first written ① .... to the Cornish pasty dates back to the thirteenth ② ....

The pasty is a pastry case containing a potato, swede, onion and minced or diced beef mixture.

In the eighteenth century the pasty was the staple ③ .... of working men in ④ ....

The miners and farm ⑤ .... found the pasty to be both portable and ⑥ .... Its pastry

⑦ .... insulated the contents and the workers' dirty hands could hold the ⑧ .... of the

pasty which could be thrown away after the pasty was eaten.

The contents were nutritious and ⑨ .... and the pasty became a popular takeaway meal

⑩ .... the country.

Cloze Wordbank Test 52

 **You have 5 minutes to complete the following section.
You have 10 questions to complete within the time given.**

Complete the passage below by choosing the correct words from the wordbank. Write each answer as a capital letter in the spaces provided.

WORDBANK

A protective	**B** observe	**C** large	**D** appropriate	**E** mostly
F feeds	**G** buries	**H** paddock	**I** visitors	**J** predators

Tortoises

Tortoises are reptiles and have scales all over their skin. They have a ①_____ shell into which

they can pull their head, legs and tail to avoid ②_____ .

Tortoises ③_____ eat vegetation but some will eat meat if they come across it. Baby tortoises

hatch from eggs which the female ④_____ underground.

The world's oldest living land creature is a giant tortoise called Jonathan who lives in the British

territory of St Helena and is estimated to be 184 years old.

He is kept in a ⑤_____ at the British Governor's residence and ⑥_____ can ⑦_____ his

movements (or lack of) from a viewing corridor, at an ⑧_____ distance.

He is looked after by his own veterinary officer, who ⑨_____ him a ⑩_____ bucket of salad

every Sunday.

DID YOU KNOW? The fastest recorded speed for a tortoise is 5 mph.

Cloze Sentences Test 53

TOP TIME MANAGEMENT TIPS

- Read the whole sentence before answering the question.
- Put in the words you know easily first of all.
- Try reading the words in the wordbank first, then the sentence. This works well for some people.

 INSTRUCTIONS

 You have 4 minutes to complete the following section.
You have 8 questions to complete within the time given.

Complete the sentences by choosing the correct word from the wordbank. Write each answer as a capital letter in the space provided.

EXAMPLE

| **A** bottle | **B** boat | **C** caravan | **D** spacecraft | **E** submarine |

If you want to travel to the moon the only way to get there is in a ① D .

The correct answer is **D** *spacecraft*.

Test 53 continues on the next page.

1. Manchester United Football Club is a professional football club .... in Old Trafford, Manchester.

| A adjacent | B proximity | C frequented | D based | E bias |

2. Dinosaurs .... on the earth millions of years ago and were the dominant terrestrials.

| A apparition | B devoured | C appeared | D promoted | E discovered |

3. A tapestry is a heavy cloth with pictures or designs that were .... by weaving or embroidery.

| A painted | B destroyed | C moulded | D managed | E formed |

4. A mangonel was a .... of catapult used in medieval times to throw projectiles at castle walls during battle.

| A monster | B type | C leaf | D machine | E tent |

5. Researchers in the USA have found .... which suggests the presence of a huge planet with a mass about ten times that of Earth.

| A evidence | B Martians | C millions | D metres | E orbits |

6. The rarest butterfly in Britain is the High Brown Fritillary which is at serious risk of .... as a result of the loss of habitats.

| A extension | B expectation | C extinction | D excitement | E elaboration |

7. Manatees are large, slow-moving .... mammals, sometimes known as sea cows, and inhabit the Caribbean Sea, the Gulf of Mexico and the Amazon Basin.

| A marine | B revine | C crescent | D crevice | E habitat |

8. Roald Dahl was a British .... who wrote many much-loved stories for children.

| A antics | B aunty | C author | D aspect | E anchovy |

Cloze Sentences Test 54

Complete the sentences below by choosing the correct word from the wordbank. Write each answer as a capital letter in the space provided.

1 Virtual reality refers to the creation of a virtual environment .... to our senses in such a way that we experience it as if we were really there.

A predicted	**B** managed	**C** contended	**D** presented	**E** blended

2 Yellowstone National Park in America is an area of outstanding .... beauty and is also a supervolcano.

A nurture	**B** nutrition	**C** nocturnal	**D** natural	**E** numerous

3 An atom is the smallest unit of matter and is mostly made up of empty ....

A space	**B** minutes	**C** moments	**D** race	**E** numbers

4 In the natural world lions live in the .... for an average of 12 years; however, in captivity they can live up to 25 years.

A loft	**B** cosmos	**C** cavern	**D** wonder	**E** wild

5 The far side of the Moon is the .... that always faces away from the Earth.

A circular	**B** rotund	**C** hemisphere	**D** planet	**E** star

6 Science fiction is a type of fiction which is based on .... science and technology.

A majestic	**B** magic	**C** logic	**D** static	**E** futuristic

7 Tea is a drink made by pouring .... water over leaves gathered from the tea plant.

A swirling	**B** leaning	**C** flooding	**D** boiling	**E** splashing

8 A tradition is a belief, legend, behaviour, custom or piece of information passed down from one .... to another.

A gentle	**B** gigantic	**C** generator	**D** gender	**E** generation

Cloze Sentences Test 55

 You have 5 minutes to complete the following section.
You have 8 questions to complete within the time given.

Complete the sentences below by choosing the correct word from the wordbank. Write each answer as a capital letter in the space provided.

(1) Most people have seen a picture of Van Gogh's painting called 'Sunflowers' but few people .... he actually painted a series of sunflower pictures.

| **A** realise | **B** release | **C** placed | **D** remorse | **E** reward |

(2) Go-karts come in all shapes and sizes, from models which are pedalled to high- .... motorised machines.

| **A** polluted | **B** pounded | **C** powered | **D** proposition | **E** prolonged |

(3) The Yeti or the Abominable Snowman is said to live in the Himalayan .... of Nepal.

| **A** religion | **B** reign | **C** regain | **D** remain | **E** region |

(4) The Lamborghini Aventador is a two-seater sports car with doors that open with an upward motion and are .... to as scissor doors.

| **A** referred | **B** resent | **C** rotate | **D** ricochet | **E** remain |

(5) High-technology swimwear fabrics are materials used for swimwear which allow competitive swimmers to .... through the water very quickly and easily.

| **A** bide | **B** glide | **C** gleam | **D** glitch | **E** bribe |

(6) A superhero is a heroic character who .... superpowers and uses these powers to combat crime.

| **A** recesses | **B** possesses | **C** fortress | **D** deflected | **E** depicted |

(7) In the Georgian era, which covered the years from 1714 to 1830, men and women often wore wigs as the fashion was to wear the hair piled up in .... styles.

| **A** elastic | **B** elliptical | **C** elaborate | **D** elated | **E** entailed |

(8) A class of children were asked what their favourite sandwich filling was and the .... were shown in a bar chart.

| **A** return | **B** menu | **C** relish | **D** radish | **E** results |

Cloze Select the Word Test 56

TOP TIME MANAGEMENT TIPS

- Read the whole passage before ticking the boxes.
- Tick the words you know easily first of all.
- If you are not sure, cross out the words you think are definitely wrong and select your best guess from the remaining words.

 INSTRUCTIONS

 You have 4 minutes to complete the following section.
You have 10 questions to complete within the time given.

Tick the correct words to complete the passage.

EXAMPLE

① ☐ taste
There are ☑ seven colours in a rainbow.
☐ zero
☐ year

The correct sentence is *There are seven colours in a rainbow.*

Test 56 continues on the next page.

Volcanoes

A volcano is a very large

① ☐ bang
☐ light
☐ danger
☐ hole

going down through the top

② ☐ liner
☐ lift
☐ layer
☐ mould

of the

③ ☐ level
☐ power
☐ part
☐ Earth

. This deep

④ ☐ box
☐ bench
☐ house
☐ shaft

allows hot

⑤ ☐ melt
☐ gases
☐ mud
☐ mixture

, ash and lava

to spew out.

The earth is made up of

⑥ ☐ three
☐ turn
☐ team
☐ through

layers: the crust, which is the outer

⑦ ☐ building
☐ surface
☐ core
☐ jelly

, the mantle and the core, which is

⑧ ☐ lead
☐ molten
☐ metal
☐ miner

rock called magma

and lies at the very

⑨ ☐ above
☐ centre
☐ lower
☐ below

of the

⑩ ☐ moon
☐ city
☐ sea
☐ planet

.

There are three ways to describe a volcano and these explain the stage of activity

of the volcano. They are: active, erupting and dormant.

DID YOU KNOW? *The name 'volcano' comes from the Roman god of fire (including volcanoes' fire), Vulcan. His festival, the Vulcanalia was celebrated annually on 23 August in the hope he would not burn the crops.*

Cloze Select the Word Test 57

Tick the correct words to complete the passage.

Marigold

Marigold was ten years old, quite tall with beautiful golden hair the

① ☐ scent
☐ coach
☐ colour
☐ cream

of marigolds. Her godmother asked her to come and stay with her for a few days

so Marigold

② ☐ denied
☐ approached
☐ agreed
☐ alone

to visit. On the first night Marigold was annoyed to

be sent to bed when the sun was still bright in the sky.

③ ☐ Reluctantly
☐ Loudly
☐ Fully
☐ Hugely

she settled

herself under the pretty

④ ☐ flower
☐ coach
☐ setting
☐ quilt

and stared at the blue sky through the open

window. Suddenly, with a

⑤ ☐ jolt
☐ broom
☐ jam
☐ bright

, Marigold felt the wooden bed lift from the

floor. She

⑥ ☐ hunched
☐ mashed
☐ wretched
☐ clutched

the sides of the

⑦ ☐ muddle
☐ mattress
☐ moor
☐ middle

as the little bed floated

smoothly out of the open

⑧ ☐ roof
☐ window
☐ tap
☐ fan

and across the garden

⑨ ☐ towards
☐ away
☐ before
☐ gentle

the

wide

⑩ ☐ explode
☐ expense
☐ explain
☐ expanse

of moorland.

Cloze Select the Word Test 58

 You have 4 minutes to complete the following section.
You have 10 questions to complete within the time given.

Tick the correct words to complete the passage.

Hadrian's Wall

In 55 BC the Roman

① ☐ coin
☐ Queen
☐ penguin
☐ emperor

Julius Caesar

② ☐ involved
☐ invaded
☐ internal
☐ intense

Britain. He wanted to

make Britain part of Rome's

③ ☐ fountain
☐ entire
☐ empire
☐ food

. However, the British fought

④ ☐ bravely
☐ quickly
☐ softly
☐ gently

and Caesar went back across the

⑤ ☐ cliffs
☐ Channel
☐ tunnel
☐ bridge

to France, which in those days

was called Gaul. He came back a year

⑥ ☐ ahead
☐ ago
☐ last
☐ later

and, even though the Britons

fought on, the Romans

⑦ ☐ reluctantly
☐ gradually
☐ instantly
☐ gracefully

moved up the country. In AD 122 the

Romans in

⑧ ☐ English
☐ South
☐ North
☐ Britain

had a new emperor called Hadrian, who

⑨ ☐ barged
☐ belt
☐ built
☐ banked

a

great wall across the north of England. The

⑩ ☐ walk
☐ wall
☐ house
☐ weather

still stands today and is

135 kilometres long and known as Hadrian's Wall.

Cloze Select the Word Test 59

 You have 3 minutes to complete the following section.
You have 10 questions to complete within the time given.

Tick the correct words to complete the passage.

Sydney Funnel-Web

① ☐ woolliest
☐ darkest
☐ densest
☐ deadliest

The _____ spider in the world lives in Australia. The Sydney funnel-web

② ☐ plenty
☐ produces
☐ buys
☐ lets

a highly toxic venom and

③ ☐ lifts
☐ injects
☐ wraps
☐ takes

this poison into its victims with

large fangs. It

④ ☐ inhabits
☐ dances
☐ eats
☐ sings

humid, sheltered places in both forests and

⑤ ☐ urchin
☐ urgent
☐ urban
☐ under

areas but can wander into

⑥ ☐ grim
☐ gardens
☐ glass
☐ people

and sometimes fall into swimming pools.

The

⑦ ☐ forehead
☐ fangs
☐ feet
☐ feelers

of this spider are larger than those of a brown snake and

the

⑧ ☐ velvet
☐ varnish
☐ victor
☐ venom

can easily kill a person. In 1981

⑨ ☐ soccer
☐ scientists
☐ plants
☐ animals

invented

⑩ ☐ anti-matter
☐ anti-gravity
☐ vicious
☐ antivenom

and so no one has died from the spider's bite since then.

Cloze Select the Word Test 60

 You have 4 minutes to complete the following section.

You have 10 questions to complete within the time given.

Tick the correct words to complete the passage.

Skateboarding

For the second time, skateboarder Danny Way has set the Guinness World Record

for the
① ☐ loveliest
☐ smartest
☐ highest
☐ brightest
air skateboard (quarter pipe).

At a
② ☐ special
☐ financial
☐ annoyed
☐ marshall
sponsored event in California, Danny
③ ☐ flattened
☐ forgot
☐ flew
☐ funded
and landed

an
④ ☐ intense
☐ incredible
☐ invisible
☐ increase
25.5 feet off a quarter pipe,
⑤ ☐ equalling
☐ failing
☐ beating
☐ losing
the previous world

record of 23.5 feet.

To
⑥ ☐ accept
☐ accomplish
☐ access
☐ accent
this
⑦ ☐ feat
☐ flew
☐ fought
☐ flap
, Danny hired a company to
⑧ ☐ build
☐ ruin
☐ wreck
☐ bruise
a

⑨ ☐ farm
☐ shop
☐ ramp
☐ staircase
256 feet long and 58 feet tall.

The ramp allowed Danny to hit speeds up to 55 mph with drop-in towers reaching

85 feet. Danny was able to
⑩ ☐ flat
☐ sky
☐ flame
☐ fly
about 81 feet above ground.

Answers

Cloze Wordbank Test 1

Q1 *B*
discovered

Q2 *H*
visit

Q3 *G*
studying

Q4 *J*
information

Q5 *D*
array

Q6 *F*
survey

Q7 *E*
entire

Q8 *A*
scrutinised

Q9 *I*
scientists

Q10 *C*
presence

Cloze Wordbank Test 2

Q1 *E*
carved

Q2 *H*
bedrock

Q3 *C*
god

Q4 *B*
symbolises

Q5 *G*
mythology

Q6 *F*
terrain

Q7 *J*
shifting

Q8 *D*
reveal

Q9 *A*
entirety

Q10 *I*
awe

Cloze Wordbank Test 3

Q1 *F*
address

Q2 *B*
buttonhole

Q3 *G*
procedure

Q4 *D*
marvel

Q5 *C*
courageous

Q6 *J*
ensuring

Q7 *I*
precious

Q8 *H*
raids

Q9 *E*
impending

Q10 *A*
safety

Cloze Wordbank Test 4

Q1 *A*
detector

Q2 *H*
metal

Q3 *J*
crumbly

Q4 *E*
anticipation

Q5 *G*
quickening

Q6 *I*
trowel

Q7 *D*
fingernail

Q8 *C*
protruding

Q9 *F*
object

Q10 *B*
cascading

Cloze Wordbank Test 5

Q1 *E*
behind

Q2 *F*
forbidden

Q3 *D*
upon

Q4 *I*
demanded

Q5 *J*
fascinating

Q6 *C*
fairies

Q7 *H*
understandably

Q8 *A*
disbelieving

Q9 *G*
camera

Q10 *B*
depicted

Cloze Wordbank Test 6

Q1 *H*
powered

Q2 *B*
leading

Q3 *M*
designed

Q4 *N*
break

Q5 *E*
record

Q6 *C*
attempt

Q7 *J*
current

Q8 *F*
extremely

Q9 *G*
disintegrate

Q10 *I*
heavy

Cloze Wordbank Test 7

Q1 *J*
built

Q2 *G*
wood

Q3 *H*
victory

Q4 *C*
protecting

Q5 *I*
kingdom

Q6 *A*
frenzy

Q7 *F*
continued

Q8 *D*
structures

Q9 *E*
permanent

Q10 *B*
early

Cloze Wordbank Test 8

Q1 *A*
butterflies

Q2 *J*
distinctive

Q3 *I*
patterned

Q4 *B*
migration

Q5 *E*
northerly

Q6 *G*
climates

Q7 *D*
travelling

Q8 *F*
journey

Q9 *C*
second

Q10 *H*
habitat

Cloze Wordbank Test 9

Q1 *D*
ceremonial

Q2 *G*
acquired

Q3 *I*
Queen

Q4 *E*
toughened

Q5 *J*
guarded

Q6 B
nicknamed

Q7 C
disguised

Q8 A
accomplices

Q9 F
apprehended

Q10 H
perpetrators

Cloze Wordbank Test 10

Q1 A
average

Q2 I
flightless

Q3 H
frigid

Q4 J
insulating

Q5 C
feathers

Q6 F
protect

Q7 G
fierce

Q8 D
conditions

Q9 B
huddle

Q10 E
groups

Cloze Wordbank Test 11

Q1 B
inhabitants

Q2 I
arrived

Q3 E
memory

Q4 C
human

Q5 F
divided

Q6 G
subject

Q7 D
knowledge

Q8 H
useful

Q9 J
inhabited

Q10 A
imprisoned

Cloze Wordbank Test 12

Q1 E
traditional

Q2 J
dessert

Q3 A
accompaniments

Q4 F
households

Q5 B
sprig

Q6 G
offer

Q7 C
douse

Q8 I
alight

Q9 D
hearty

Q10 H
mixture

Cloze Wordbank Test 13

Q1 H
commonly

Q2 E
represent

Q3 A
credited

Q4 B
legend

Q5 J
travels

Q6 D
hermit

Q7 I
living

Q8 G
demanded

Q9 C
sacrifice

Q10 F
maiden

Cloze Wordbank Test 14

Q1 *I*
painter

Q2 *D*
talents

Q3 *F*
particularly

Q4 *A*
created

Q5 *E*
machines

Q6 *C*
resembled

Q7 *B*
expert

Q8 *G*
anatomy

Q9 *J*
detailed

Q10 *H*
observations

Cloze Wordbank Test 15

Q1 *E*
longships

Q2 *J*
plunder

Q3 *H*
adventurers

Q4 *B*
Norway

Q5 *I*
North

Q6 *F*
coasts

Q7 *G*
evidence

Q8 *K*
exists

Q9 *M*
common

Q10 *D*
woodland

Cloze Wordbank Test 16

Q1 *A*
unlike

Q2 *F*
pictures

Q3 *D*
three

Q4 *B*
dimensional

Q5 *J*
depth

Q6 *H*
object

Q7 *I*
light

Q8 *E*
bounces

Q9 *C*
piece

Q10 *G*
captures

Cloze Wordbank Test 17

Q1 *I*
author

Q2 *E*
visited

Q3 *B*
browsing

Q4 *H*
second

Q5 *F*
bought

Q6 *D*
eagerly

Q7 *J*
much

Q8 *G*
upon

Q9 *A*
spotted

Q10 *C*
name

Cloze Wordbank Test 18

Q1 *G*
famous

Q2 *A*
launched

Q3 *E*
partake

Q4 *H*
afternoon

Q5 *I*
exercise

Q6 B
turn

Q7 D
debt

Q8 J
saved

Q9 F
match

Q10 C
donations

Cloze Wordbank Test 19

Q1 B
rechargeable

Q2 A
typically

Q3 F
arranged

Q4 G
positions

Q5 C
device

Q6 E
pressure

Q7 I
developed

Q8 H
popular

Q9 D
popularity

Q10 J
attributed

Cloze Wordbank Test 20

Q1 D
million

Q2 F
digesting

Q3 G
growing

Q4 J
knowledge

Q5 E
travels

Q6 A
gold

Q7 C
metals

Q8 B
bodies

Q9 H
exercise

Q10 I
muscles

Cloze Wordbank Test 21

Q1 B
consisting

Q2 H
served

Q3 E
pre-cooked

Q4 D
spread

Q5 F
arrange

Q6 C
roll

Q7 J
firmly

Q8 A
cut

Q9 G
process

Q10 I
require

Cloze Wordbank Test 22

Q1 C
temporary

Q2 F
reconstructed

Q3 H
year

Q4 G
experience

Q5 I
temperatures

Q6 J
visitors

Q7 A
bedrooms

Q8 D
deer

Q9 E
sleeping

Q10 B
instead

Cloze Wordbank Test 23

Q1 N
adrift

Q2 J
describe

Q3 G
survive

Q4 I
captured

Q5 C
escape

Q6 F
captors

Q7 D
briefly

Q8 A
dense

Q9 K
managed

Q10 O
rescued

Cloze Wordbank Test 24

Q1 H
communities

Q2 E
identified

Q3 G
necessary

Q4 B
information

Q5 I
original

Q6 A
surname

Q7 D
introduce

Q8 F
passed

Q9 J
adopted

Q10 C
hereditary

Cloze Wordbank Test 25

Q1 H
invented

Q2 D
accident

Q3 G
attended

Q4 E
frustrating

Q5 B
listening

Q6 J
code

Q7 A
raised

Q8 C
represented

Q9 I
fingertips

Q10 F
signs

Cloze Wordbank Test 26

Q1 E
people

Q2 G
region

Q3 A
marker

Q4 H
landmarks

Q5 F
typically

Q6 C
person

Q7 J
stretched

Q8 B
carefully

Q9 I
Canada

Q10 D
featured

Cloze Wordbank Test 27

Q1 D
goddess

Q2 E
believed

Q3 G
homes

Q4 H
design

Q5 C
celebration

Q6 I
symbols

Q7 J
infinity

Q8 A
lotus

Q9 F
drawn

Q10 B
indicate

Cloze Wordbank Test 28

Q1 F
receives

Q2 I
recognition

Q3 D
need

Q4 B
risk

Q5 H
tirelessly

Q6 C
environment

Q7 E
challenges

Q8 G
examples

Q9 J
volunteer

Q10 A
single

Cloze Wordbank Test 29

Q1 I
satisfaction

Q2 F
hundreds

Q3 C
energetic

Q4 B
body

Q5 D
requires

Q6 J
manipulate

Q7 H
thread

Q8 E
popular

Q9 A
activities

Q10 G
unusual

Cloze Wordbank Test 30

Q1 H
produce

Q2 F
undigested

Q3 B
bones

Q4 C
within

Q5 J
vegetable

Q6 A
contents

Q7 D
identified

Q8 G
hunting

Q9 E
number

Q10 I
period

Cloze Wordbank Test 31

Q1 L
parcel

Q2 M
carried

Q3 H
plague

Q4 B
villagers

Q5 O
decision

Q6 I
disease

Q7 C
north

Q8 E
outside

Q9 F
death

Q10 A
brave

Cloze Wordbank Test 32

Q1 E
blazer

Q2 G
brown

Q3 H
adjusted

Q4 J
stature

Q5 F
smell

Q6 C
lessen

Q7 B
replenished
Q8 A
bulging
Q9 D
pencil
Q10 I
ink

Cloze Wordbank Test 33

Q1 H
separating
Q2 A
suspended
Q3 D
steps
Q4 F
avoiding
Q5 I
obstructions
Q6 C
passengers
Q7 B
mainland
Q8 J
turns
Q9 E
exposes
Q10 G
causeway

Cloze Wordbank Test 34

Q1 H
loch
Q2 D
lake
Q3 F
deepest
Q4 G
attracts
Q5 E
appreciating
Q6 J
scenery
Q7 B
Monster
Q8 C
reputedly
Q9 I
conclusive

Q10 A
myth

Cloze Wordbank Test 35

Q1 G
evergreen
Q2 C
celebrate
Q3 E
fragrant
Q4 A
months
Q5 I
believed
Q6 J
traditionally
Q7 H
origins
Q8 F
preach
Q9 D
worshipping
Q10 B
chopped

Cloze Wordbank Test 36

Q1 H
century
Q2 E
characters
Q3 A
villain
Q4 G
plot
Q5 D
fairy
Q6 C
traced
Q7 F
theme
Q8 B
festival
Q9 J
opposite
Q10 I
reflect

Cloze Wordbank Test 37

Q1 G
referred

Q2 **J**
mainly

Q3 **F**
breed

Q4 **B**
highly

Q5 **E**
energetic

Q6 **I**
shepherds

Q7 **C**
requires

Q8 **A**
stimulation

Q9 **H**
physical

Q10 **D**
owner

Cloze Wordbank Test 38

Q1 **A**
species

Q2 **I**
prey

Q3 **C**
landing

Q4 **B**
puncture

Q5 **E**
tongue

Q6 **F**
wound

Q7 **D**
aware

Q8 **H**
spread

Q9 **J**
diseases

Q10 **G**
infected

Cloze Wordbank Test 39

Q1 **H**
character

Q2 **J**
version

Q3 **A**
played

Q4 **E**
several

Q5 **B**
survived

Q6 **C**
stolen

Q7 **I**
original

Q8 **F**
silver

Q9 **D**
advantage

Q10 **G**
era

Cloze Wordbank Test 40

Q1 **F**
capital

Q2 **C**
school

Q3 **J**
reason

Q4 **A**
avoid

Q5 **B**
jams

Q6 **H**
journey

Q7 **E**
ranked

Q8 **G**
worst

Q9 **D**
hours

Q10 **I**
stranded

Cloze Wordbank Test 41

Q1 **A**
Wednesday

Q2 **D**
early

Q3 **I**
chores

Q4 **E**
water

Q5 **F**
ends

Q6 **B**
lessons

Q7 **H**
different

Q8   C
students
Q9   G
clean
Q10 J
leaving

Cloze Wordbank Test 42

Q1   H
categorised
Q2   A
baby
Q3   D
given
Q4   J
between
Q5   F
under
Q6   E
grown
Q7   B
respectively
Q8   I
regardless
Q9   C
gender
Q10 G
animal

Cloze Wordbank Test 43

Q1   D
spacecraft
Q2   H
leaving
Q3   J
comet
Q4   A
bumpy
Q5   C
hidden
Q6   B
power
Q7   I
transmit
Q8   E
Earth
Q9   F
sunlight
Q10 G
panels

Cloze Wordbank Test 44

Q1   E
involves
Q2   C
climbing
Q3   G
giant
Q4   I
challenging
Q5   A
sometimes
Q6   F
venues
Q7   H
country
Q8   D
soccer
Q9   J
variation
Q10 B
combines

Cloze Wordbank Test 45

Q1   F
imagination
Q2   N
sprinkle
Q3   M
represent
Q4   E
carefully
Q5   O
picked
Q6   C
baskets
Q7   I
pond
Q8   B
admired
Q9   A
reflected
Q10 H
shiny

Cloze Wordbank Test 46

Q1   E
kangaroo
Q2   A
colonised
Q3   I
colony

Q4 **B**
bred

Q5 **F**
pair

Q6 **J**
incident

Q7 **D**
reports

Q8 **G**
loose

Q9 **H**
advice

Q10 **C**
roam

Cloze Wordbank Test 47

Q1 **G**
inspired

Q2 **E**
recreational

Q3 **A**
winter

Q4 **I**
techniques

Q5 **F**
developed

Q6 **B**
describe

Q7 **J**
involves

Q8 **D**
performing

Q9 **H**
clothing

Q10 **C**
appropriate

Cloze Wordbank Test 48

Q1 **E**
formations

Q2 **A**
spike

Q3 **G**
formed

Q4 **C**
drip

Q5 **I**
down

Q6 **J**
commonly

Q7 **D**
caves

Q8 **B**
easy

Q9 **F**
remember

Q10 **H**
refers

Cloze Wordbank Test 49

Q1 **I**
physical

Q2 **A**
swimmer

Q3 **G**
tumbles

Q4 **J**
riverbed

Q5 **D**
towering

Q6 **F**
inflatable

Q7 **B**
rapidly

Q8 **H**
allows

Q9 **C**
surfaces

Q10 **E**
participants

Cloze Wordbank Test 50

Q1 **A**
enjoy

Q2 **J**
healthy

Q3 **H**
dancing

Q4 **G**
everyone

Q5 **E**
suits

Q6 **F**
classical

Q7 **I**
modern

Q8 **C**
partner

Q9 **B**
creative

Q10 **D**
funky

Cloze Wordbank Test 51

Q1 **B**
reference
Q2 **H**
century
Q3 **I**
diet
Q4 **E**
Cornwall
Q5 **A**
workers
Q6 **G**
convenient
Q7 **F**
case
Q8 **J**
crusts
Q9 **C**
filling
Q10 **D**
throughout

Cloze Wordbank Test 52

Q1 **A**
protective
Q2 **J**
predators
Q3 **E**
mostly
Q4 **G**
buries
Q5 **H**
paddock
Q6 **I**
visitors
Q7 **B**
observe
Q8 **D**
appropriate
Q9 **F**
feeds
Q10 **C**
large

Cloze Sentences Test 53

Q1 **D** based   **Q5** **A** evidence
Q2 **C** appeared   **Q6** **C** extinction
Q3 **E** formed   **Q7** **A** marine
Q4 **B** type   **Q8** **C** author

Cloze Sentences Test 54

Q1 **D** presented   **Q5** **C** hemisphere
Q2 **D** natural   **Q6** **E** futuristic
Q3 **A** space   **Q7** **D** boiling
Q4 **E** wild   **Q8** **E** generation

Cloze Sentences Test 55

Q1 **A** realise   **Q5** **B** glide
Q2 **C** powered   **Q6** **B** possesses
Q3 **E** region   **Q7** **C** elaborate
Q4 **A** referred   **Q8** **E** results

Cloze Select the Word Test 56

Q1 hole   **Q6** three
Q2 layer   **Q7** surface
Q3 Earth   **Q8** molten
Q4 shaft   **Q9** centre
Q5 gases   **Q10** planet

Cloze Select the Word Test 57

Q1 colour   **Q6** clutched
Q2 agreed   **Q7** mattress
Q3 Reluctantly   **Q8** window
Q4 quilt   **Q9** towards
Q5 jolt   **Q10** expanse

Cloze Select the Word Test 58

Q1 emperor   **Q6** later
Q2 invaded   **Q7** gradually
Q3 empire   **Q8** Britain
Q4 bravely   **Q9** built
Q5 Channel   **Q10** wall

Cloze Select the Word Test 59

Q1 deadliest   **Q6** gardens
Q2 produces   **Q7** fangs
Q3 injects   **Q8** venom
Q4 inhabits   **Q9** scientists
Q5 urban   **Q10** antivenom

Cloze Select the Word Test 60

Q1 highest   **Q6** accomplish
Q2 special   **Q7** feat
Q3 flew   **Q8** build
Q4 incredible   **Q9** ramp
Q5 beating   **Q10** fly

Score Sheet

Below is a score sheet to track your results over multiple attempts. One mark is available for each question in the tests.

Test	Pages	Date of first attempt	Score	Date of second attempt	Score	Date of third attempt	Score
Cloze Wordbank Test 1	4–5						
Cloze Wordbank Test 2	6						
Cloze Wordbank Test 3	7						
Cloze Wordbank Test 4	8						
Cloze Wordbank Test 5	9						
Cloze Wordbank Test 6	10						
Cloze Wordbank Test 7	11						
Cloze Wordbank Test 8	12						
Cloze Wordbank Test 9	13						
Cloze Wordbank Test 10	14						
Cloze Wordbank Test 11	15						
Cloze Wordbank Test 12	16						
Cloze Wordbank Test 13	17						
Cloze Wordbank Test 14	18						
Cloze Wordbank Test 15	19						
Cloze Wordbank Test 16	20						
Cloze Wordbank Test 17	21						
Cloze Wordbank Test 18	22						
Cloze Wordbank Test 19	23						
Cloze Wordbank Test 20	24						
Cloze Wordbank Test 21	25						
Cloze Wordbank Test 22	26						
Cloze Wordbank Test 23	27						
Cloze Wordbank Test 24	28						
Cloze Wordbank Test 25	29						
Cloze Wordbank Test 26	30						
Cloze Wordbank Test 27	31						
Cloze Wordbank Test 28	32						

Test	Pages	Date of first attempt	Score	Date of second attempt	Score	Date of third attempt	Score
Cloze Wordbank Test 29	33						
Cloze Wordbank Test 30	34						
Cloze Wordbank Test 31	35						
Cloze Wordbank Test 32	36						
Cloze Wordbank Test 33	37						
Cloze Wordbank Test 34	38						
Cloze Wordbank Test 35	39						
Cloze Wordbank Test 36	40						
Cloze Wordbank Test 37	41						
Cloze Wordbank Test 38	42						
Cloze Wordbank Test 39	43						
Cloze Wordbank Test 40	44						
Cloze Wordbank Test 41	45						
Cloze Wordbank Test 42	46						
Cloze Wordbank Test 43	47						
Cloze Wordbank Test 44	48						
Cloze Wordbank Test 45	49						
Cloze Wordbank Test 46	50						
Cloze Wordbank Test 47	51						
Cloze Wordbank Test 48	52						
Cloze Wordbank Test 49	53						
Cloze Wordbank Test 50	54						
Cloze Wordbank Test 51	55						
Cloze Wordbank Test 52	56						
Cloze Sentences Test 53	57–58						
Cloze Sentences Test 54	59						
Cloze Sentences Test 55	60						
Cloze Select the Word Test 56	61–62						
Cloze Select the Word Test 57	63						
Cloze Select the Word Test 58	64						
Cloze Select the Word Test 59	65						
Cloze Select the Word Test 60	66						